MW00593119

INTERIORS BY COLOR

INTERIEURS UND FARBEN
INTÉRIEURS PAR COULEUR
INTERIEURS OP KLEUR

Edited by Macarena San Martín

Art director:
Mireia Casanovas Soley

Editorial coordination:
Simone Schleifer

Project coordination:
Macarena San Martín

Texts:
Macarena San Martín

Layout:
Yolanda G. Román

Translations coordination: Equipo de Edición, Barcelona.
Translations: Heike Reissig, Bonalingua Übersetzungen (German), Rachel Burden (English), Anne Dumail (French), Tanja Timmerman (Dutch)

Editorial project:
2008 © LOFT Publications | Via Laietana, 32, 4.°, Of. 92 | 08003 Barcelona, Spain
Tel.: +34 932 688 088 Fax: +34 932 687 073 | loft@loftpublications.com | www.loftpublications.com

ISBN 978-84-96936-20-1   Printed in China

Cover photos/Back cover photos: © Jordi Sarrà

LOFT affirms that it possesses all the necessary rights for the publication of this material and has duly paid all royalties related to the authors' and photographers' rights. LOFT also affirms that it has violated no property rights and has respected common law, all authors' rights and other rights that could be relevant. Finally, LOFT affirms that this book contains no obscene nor slanderous material.

The total or partial reproduction of this book without the authorization of the publishers violates the two rights reserved; any use must be requested in advance.

If you would like to propose works to include in our upcoming books, please email us at loft@loftpublications.com.

In some cases it has been impossible to locate copyright owners of the images published in this book. Please contact the publisher if you are the copyright owner of any of the images published here.

INTERIORS BY COLOR

INTERIEURS UND FARBEN
INTÉRIEURS PAR COULEUR
INTERIEURS OP KLEUR

Edited by Macarena San Martín

KOLON

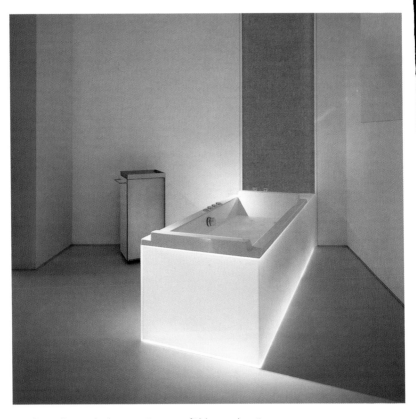

„Farbe sollte gedacht, geträumt, gefühlt werden."

Henri Matisse, französischer Maler und Begründer des Fauvismus

"Color should be thought, dreamt, imagined."

Henri Matisse, French painter and creator of Fauvism

« La couleur doit être pensée, rêvée, imaginée. »

Henri Matisse, peintre français, créateur du fauvisme

"Kleur moet worden gedacht, gedroomd, ingebeeld."

Henri Matisse, Frans schilder en een van de grondleggers van het fauvisme

Gelb ist eine leuchtende und auffällige Farbe, deren Einsatz problematisch sein kann, da man sich an ihr schnell satt sieht. Daher empfiehlt sich ein maßvoller Gebrauch bei genauer Überlegung, wo und wie sie eingesetzt werden soll. Ein weniger intensives doch warmes Gelb eignet sich nicht nur für Schlaf-, Kinder-, Wohn- und Esszimmer, sondern auch für Bäder und Küchen.

Yellow is a difficult color to use as, being cheerful and striking, one tends to tire of it quickly. It should therefore be used in moderation and after careful thought about where and how it is to be applied. A pale but warm shade is suitable for bedrooms, both children's and adults', as well as for living rooms, dining rooms and even bathrooms and kitchens.

Le jaune est une couleur difficile à utiliser car elle est si vive et gaie qu'elle a tendance à vite lasser. C'est pourquoi il ne faut pas en abuser et bien réfléchir bien au lieu et à la façon de l'appliquer. Un ton clair mais chaud est tout à fait approprié dans les chambres d'enfants et d'adultes, ou les salons, salles à manger, et même salles de bain et cuisines.

Geel is een moeilijke kleur in het gebruik; het is vrolijk en opvallend, maar verveelt snel. Geel dient met mate gebruikt te worden en pas na zorgvuldige overweging over hoe en waar. Een lichte, warme geeltint is geschikt voor slaapkamers, zowel voor kinderen als voor volwassenen, en ook voor woonkamers, eetkamers en zelfs badkamers en keukens.

Orange ist eine kräftige, optimistische Farbe, die sehr vital wirkt, da sie die Energie und Intensität von Rot und Gelb in sich vereint. Vor allem Details lassen sich mit Orangetönen gekonnt in Szene setzen. Orange lässt sich ideal mit anderen Farben kombinieren, am besten in Schlafzimmern oder Küchen, oder aber in Wohnräumen, die viel Tageslicht haben.

Orange is a daring color radiating vitality and optimism, and has the energy and intensity of red and yellow. Any detail in a home can take touches of orange and be pleasing to the eye. It is ideal to combine with other colors and to use in all rooms such as bedrooms or kitchens, or areas with plenty of natural light.

L'orange est une couleur osée qui dégage vitalité et optimisme. Elle a l'énergie et l'intensité du rouge et du jaune. Dans la maison, n'importe quel détail peut avoir des touches d'orange et être agréable à voir. C'est une couleur idéale à combiner à d'autres couleurs dans des pièces comme les chambres, les cuisines ou les espaces qui reçoivent une abondante lumière naturelle.

Oranje is een gedurfde kleur die vitaliteit en optimisme uitstraalt. Oranje heeft dezelfde energie en intensiteit als rood en geel. Het is geschikt voor elk detail in huis en is prettig voor het oog. Oranje is uitstekend te combineren met andere kleuren en leent zich voor allerlei vertrekken, zoals slaapkamers, keukens en andere ruimten met veel daglicht.

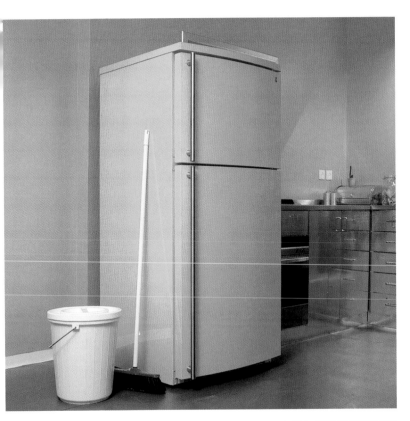

45

Rot ist die Farbe der Leidenschaft, eine kräftige Primärfarbe mit Charakter. Sie sollte stets maßvoll eingesetzt werden, an nur einer Wand oder in Kinderzimmern. Da Rot mit Wärme und Lebendigkeit assoziiert wird, lässt sich diese Farbe in Sommerhäusern wesentlich freier und vielseitiger verwenden; dort schafft sie oft in ganz unterschiedlichen Räumen eine wundervolle Atmosphäre.

Red is a passionate primary color which has character and visual strength. It is generally applied in moderation, on just one wall of a room, or in children's bedrooms. In summer houses, because of its association with warm, vibrant cultures, it is used much more freely in all kinds of rooms to create wonderful atmospheres.

Le rouge est une couleur primaire passionnée, qui a du caractère et de la force visuelle. On l'utilise généralement avec modération, sur un seul mur de la pièce, ou dans les chambres d'enfants. Associée aux cultures chaudes et vibrantes, elle s'utilise beaucoup plus librement dans les maisons de vacances, où elle crée des ambiances fantastiques.

Rood is een gepassioneerde primaire kleur met karakter en visuele kracht. Het wordt doorgaans met mate gebruikt, bijvoorbeeld op één muur of in een kinderkamer. Door de associatie van rood met warme, levendige culturen wordt rood in zomerhuizen veel vrijer toegepast in allerlei vertrekken, wat prachtige sferen tot gevolg heeft.

Rosa wird gern mit Reinheit, Kindheit, Unschuld und Weiblichkeit assoziiert, weshalb diese Farbe oft in Mädchenzimmern zum Einsatz kommt. Doch es sollte nicht vergessen werden, dass Rosa sich auf eine breite Palette von Farbtönen erstreckt, die auch eine ganz andere Wirkungen entfalten können, um bei der Dekoration sehr moderne Akzente zu setzen.

Pink is associated with subtlety, childhood, purity and femininity, which is why it is often seen in little girls' or teenage girls' bedrooms. But pink should not be thought of only in this innocent way, as it has a wide range of shades that produce good chromatic quality and which, when used in decoration, add a contemporary touch.

Le rose s'associe à la délicatesse, l'enfance, la pureté et la féminité, raison pour laquelle il est fréquent de le trouver dans les chambres des petites filles ou des adolescentes. Mais le rose n'est pas seulement une couleur innocente. Son large éventail de tonalités donne à la décoration une note contemporaine.

Roze wordt geassocieerd met subtiliteit, kinderjaren, puurheid en vrouwelijkheid en is daardoor een veel gebruikte kleur in meisjesslaapkamers. Maar roze is niet alleen maar zoet en onschuldig; het heeft een breed gamma van kleurschakeringen met mooie eigenschappen die een inrichting iets eigentijds kunnen geven.

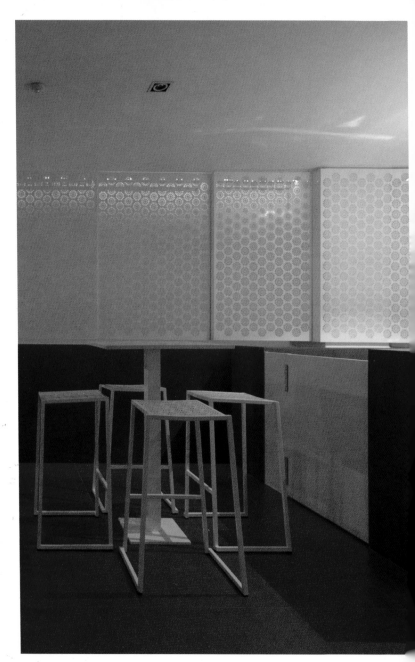

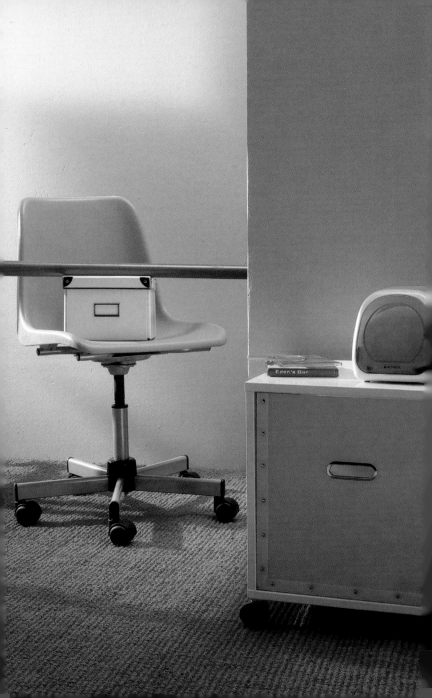

Violett ist eine mystische, königliche Farbe, die historisch mit Macht assoziiert wird. Obwohl Violett angenehm wirkt, sollte diese Farbe nicht auf großen Flächen oder als einzige Farbe im Raum eingesetzt werden, da sie sonst zu stark dominiert. Um eine ausgleichende Wirkung zu erzielen, empfiehlt sich ihre Kombination mit kontrastierenden Farben.

Violet is a mystical color which has an historical association with royalty and is very powerful. Although it is an extremely pleasant color it is important not to apply it to large surfaces or as the only color in a room since it can be a little overwhelming. Combining it with contrasting colors creates better visual balance in a space.

e violet est une couleur mystique, très
uissante, associée dans l'histoire à la
oyauté. Bien que ce soit une couleur
gréable, il faut veiller à ne pas l'appliquer
ur de grandes surfaces ou comme couleur
nique d'une pièce car le résultat pourrait
tre dérangeant. Combiné à des couleurs
ranchées, on obtient un meilleur équilibre
isuel là où il est appliqué.

Paars is een mystieke, krachtige kleur met
van oudsher koninklijke associaties.
Hoewel paars een buitengewoon
aangename kleur is, is het beter deze niet
voor al te grote oppervlakken of als enige
kleur in een vertrek te gebruiken, omdat
dat nogal overweldigend kan zijn. Een
combinatie met contrasterende kleuren
geeft een betere visuele balans in een
vertrek.

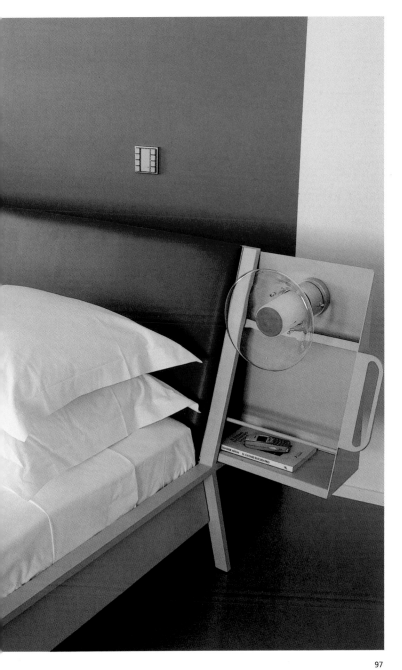

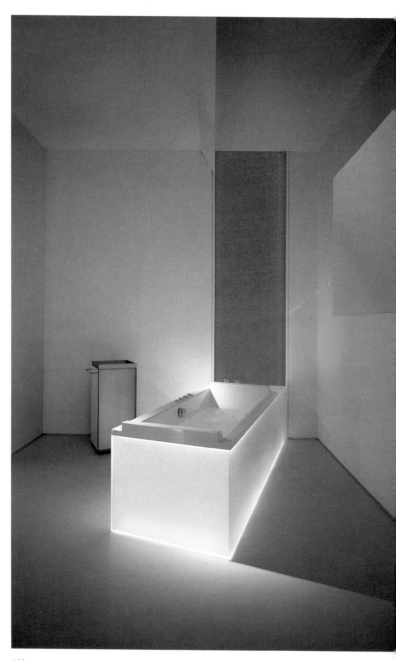

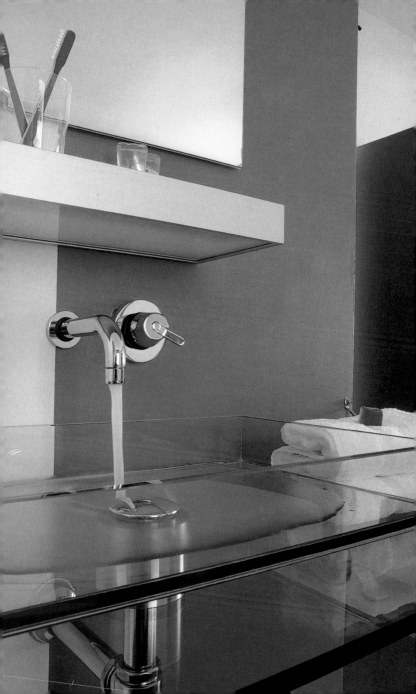

Blau ist eine der wenigen Farben, die sich problemlos überall im Haus verwenden lässt. Das Einzige, worauf geachtet werden sollte, ist die Intensität der Leuchtkraft, damit der Farbton mit dem Raum harmoniert. Da Blau über eine große Palette an Farbtönen verfügt, wird es oft in Bädern, Schlafräumen, Esszimmern, auf Holz und auch anderweitig eingesetzt.

Blue is one of the few colors which can be used without problems in any part of a house. The only thing to bear in mind is the intensity of the brightness to ensure that it harmonizes with the room. A color with a wide range of tones, it is often used in bathrooms, bedrooms, dining rooms, or wood and in many other places.

bleu est une des rares couleurs qui peut
utiliser sans problème dans toutes les
èces d'une maison. Il suffit de tenir
ompte de son intensité et fonction de la
èce où il va être utilisé. Son large éventail
e tonalités permet de l'employer dans les
lles de bain, chambres, salles à manger,
et avec du bois.

Blauw is een van de kleuren die zonder
problemen in elk vertrek van het huis
gebruikt kunnen worden. Het enige waar
rekening mee moet worden gehouden, is
de intensiteit van de kleur, zodat deze
harmonieert met de kamer. Blauw is er in
zeer uiteenlopende schakeringen en wordt
daarom gebruikt in badkamers,
slaapkamers, eetkamers, op hout en op
veel andere plaatsen.

Grün ist eine Farbe mit einer großen Vielfalt an Tönen. Alle Arten von Räumen, vom Schlafzimmer bis zum Bad, lassen sich in Grün gestalten; es kommt nur darauf an, die richtigen Töne zu wählen. Die Pastelltöne werden oft für Kacheln in Küchen oder Bädern verwendet und bieten zahlreiche Möglichkeiten in Kombination mit dunkleren Grüntönen.

Green is a color with a wide variety of h which means that any room, from the bedroom to the bathroom, can be paint this color; it is just a question of choosin the right shades. The pastel tones are generally used for tiles in kitchens and bathrooms, and offer numerous possibilities when combined with deepe greens.

vert possède une grande variété de
nalités, et on peut donc peindre
importe quelle pièce, chambre ou salle
e bain, de cette couleur. Il faut juste
hoisir la bonne gamme. Les tons pastels
emploient généralement pour les
arreaux de cuisine et salle de bain, et
ermettent de nombreuses combinaisons
ec d'autres verts plus intenses.

Groen bestaat in tal van schakeringen en is
daardoor geschikt voor de meest
uiteenlopende ruimten, van slaapkamer tot
badkamer. Het is gewoon een kwestie van
de juiste tint kiezen. De pasteltinten
worden veel gebruikt voor keuken- en
badkamertegels en bieden volop
mogelijkheden in combinatie met diepere
groentinten.

Braun lässt sich äußerst vielseitig einsetzen, denn es ist die Farbe der Natur. Braun ist vermutlich die einzige Farbe, die sowohl bei modernen als auch bei klassischen Inneneinrichtungen verwendet werden kann, sei es als Wandfarbe oder für Möbel und Accessoires. Braun harmoniert perfekt mit anderen erdigen oder neutralen Tönen und ebenso mit Blau, Grün, Rosa, Orange und Rot.

Brown has endless possibilities because it nature's own color. It is probably the only color which can be used in contemporary as well as classical houses, and for furniture or accessories. It combines perfectly with other earth and neutral tones, as well as with blue, green, pink, orange and red.

marron étant la couleur même de la ...ture, il offre de nombreuses possibilités. ...st sans doute la seule couleur qui rend ...ssi bien dans un style contemporain que ...ssique, pour le mobilier ou les ...cessoires. Il s'assortit parfaitement aux ...tres tons terre et neutres, ainsi qu'au ...u, vert, rose, orange et rouge.

Bruin heeft eindeloos veel mogelijkheden, omdat het een natuurlijke kleur is. Het is waarschijnlijk de enige kleur die het goed doet in zowel moderne als klassieke huizen en die bovendien zeer geschikt is voor meubels en accessoires. Bruin laat zich perfect combineren met andere aardetinten en tinten als blauw, groen, roze, oranje en rood.

Beige ist eine schlichte, subtile, elegante und klassische Farbe, deren chromatische Skala perfekt mit sämtlichen Brauntönen und mit Schwarz harmoniert. In Kombination mit Pastelltönen verleiht Beige diesen mehr Intensität. Beige wird häufig bei Stoffen eingesetzt und trägt maßgeblich zur warmen Wirkung von Interieurs bei.

Beige is a subtle, sophisticated, elegant, distinguished and anachronistic color. It chromatic scale adapts, with great precision and harmony, to the whole ra of browns and to black, and combining with pastel shades affords them greater character. It is a color often employed ir textiles and its use is essential in creatin warm interiors.

e beige est une couleur subtile et
ophistiquée, élégante, distinguée et
nachronique. Sa gamme chromatique
'adapte avec précision et harmonie à tous
es marrons et au noir. Il donne beaucoup
e caractère aux couleurs pastel. Le beige
st très employé dans le textile et c'est une
ouleur indispensable pour créer des
mbiances chaleureuses.

Beige is een subtiele, verfijnde, elegante,
geraffineerde en tijdloze kleur die zich
precies en harmonieus aanpast aan alle
bruin- en zwarttinten. Een combinatie met
pasteltinten versterkt het karakter van
beige. Beige wordt veel gebruikt in stoffen
en om warme interieurs te creëren.

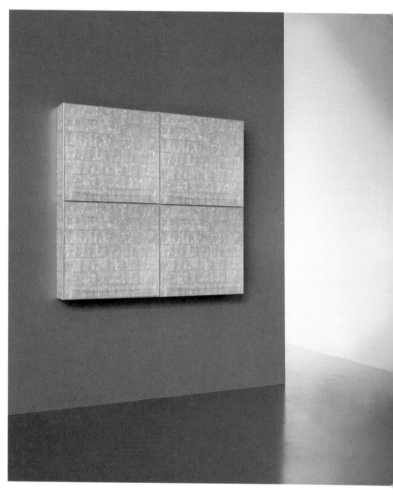

Grau sorgt innerhalb der Farbenfamilie für Ausgeglichenheit. Grau harmoniert perfekt mit allen anderen Farben, lässt sich hervorragend mit ihnen kombinieren und stabilisiert ihre Wirkung. In der Innenarchitektur spielt Grau deshalb seit jeher eine große Rolle. Oft wird Grau anstelle von Schwarz eingesetzt, um eine weniger intensive, doch ebenso elegante Wirkung zu erzielen.

Grey is the balance within the chromatic family. It is a color which stabilizes the tones applied in any space and combines perfectly and harmoniously with all colors which is why it has always been fundamental in interior design. It is frequently used as a substitute for black in order to achieve a sophisticated but less intense effect.

ns la famille des couleurs, le gris est
quilibre. C'est une couleur qui stabilise
s tons dans tous les espaces et s'assortit
rfaitement à toutes les couleurs, raison
ur laquelle elle a toujours été une
uleur basique en décoration. Elle
mplace souvent le noir quand on
cherche un effet sophistiqué pas trop
tense.

Grijs geeft balans in een kleurig geheel.
Het is een kleur die de in een ruimte
toegepaste tinten stabiliseert en
harmonieus samengaat met eigenlijk alle
kleuren, waardoor hij altijd een
prominente rol heeft gespeeld in het
interieurontwerp. Grijs wordt vaak
gebruikt als vervanger voor zwart om een
geraffineerd maar wat minder sterk effect
te krijgen.

Schwarz ist eine Farbe, die mit vielen Vorurteilen behaftet ist. In der Architektur und Inneneinrichtung wird Schwarz aufgrund seiner ästhetischen Wirkung jedoch schon immer gern eingesetzt. Schwarz wirkt modern, setzt klare Akzente und lässt sich perfekt mit zahlreichen anderen Farben kombinieren.

There is a lot of prejudice against black, but in spite of this it is absolutely essentia in interior design and architecture, where is always in vogue. As well as its aesthetic impact, it is a graphic color by nature; it guides and clearly organizes spaces as we as offering endless possibilities and combining unequivocally with the entire chromatic range.

...xiste de nombreux à priori sur cette
...uleur. Pourtant elle est absolument
...entielle et toujours à la mode dans la
...coration et l'architecture. Outre son
...pact esthétique, c'est une couleur
...aphique par nature, elle oriente et
...ganise clairement les espaces, offre des
...ssibilités sans fin et peut se combiner
...ns se tromper avec l'ensemble de la
...mme chromatique.

Ondanks de vele vooroordelen tegen zwart
is deze kleur onmisbaar en altijd in beeld in
interieurontwerp en architectuur. Los van
zijn esthetische kant is zwart van nature
een grafische kleur. Zwart is duidelijk en
organiseert ruimten en is daarnaast met
werkelijk elke andere kleur te combineren.

Weiß ist, symbolisch betrachtet, die perfekte Farbe, die Königin der Farben. Sie ist zweifellos die Farbe, die in der Innenarchitektur am häufigsten eingesetzt wird: Weiß lässt Räume heller und größer wirken, kann als neutrale Farbe mit allen anderen Farben kombiniert werden und besitzt zudem genug Präsenz, um auch allein bestehen zu können.

White is, symbolically, the most perfect color, the sum of all colors. It is, without any doubt, the most used in interior de because of the effects it produces: it illuminates rooms and makes them look bigger, it is neutral enough to combine with any other color and has sufficient presence to be used by itself.

on le symbolisme, le blanc est la couleur plus parfaite, la somme de toutes les uleurs. C'est sans aucun doute la plus isée en décoration grâce aux avantages 'elle présente : elle illumine les pièces et agrandit l'espace, elle est suffisamment utre pour se combiner à toutes les tres couleurs et assez présente pour être isée seule.

Wit is symbolisch de meest perfecte kleur. Het is zonder enige twijfel de meest gebruikte kleur in het interieurontwerp vanwege het effect dat hij heeft: wit maakt de ruimte lichter en groter, is neutraal genoeg om met elke andere kleur samen te gaan en is sterk genoeg als op zichzelf staande kleur.

Die Kombination von Farben, vor allem von leuchtenden Farben, stellt eine besondere Herausforderung dar. Richtig gemacht, kann sie zu spektakulären Ergebnissen führen. Mit der Zeit erwirbt man ein Gespür dafür, wie Farben miteinander reagieren. In der Natur und auch im Alltag lässt sich das Zusammenspiel der Farben am besten beobachten.

Mixing colors, especially bright ones, is a daring but risky undertaking. However when done properly, the result can be spectacular. Over time onelearns how colors interact, whether in nature-which is the best laboratory in which to observe them-or in daily life, where many colors come together effortlessly

mélange des couleurs, surtout lorsqu'il
git de couleurs vives, est une tâche
dacieuse qui n'est pas sans risque. Mais
résultats peuvent être spectaculaires.
ec le temps, on apprend à observer les
eractions entre les couleurs, par exemple
ns la nature, qui est le meilleur
oratoire, ou dans la vie quotidienne.

Kleuren combineren, vooral felle, is een
gedurfde maar riskante onderneming.
Indien goed gedaan, kan het resultaat
spectaculair zijn. Mettertijd leer je hoe
kleuren op elkaar inwerken, of dat nu in
de natuur is – de beste plek om ze te
observeren – of in het dagelijks leven, waar
veel kleuren moeiteloos samenkomen.

PHOTOGRAPHIC DIRECTORY

© **Jordi Sarrá**
pg. 12, 16, 18-19, 20, 31, 32, 38, 44 50,51,54-55, 64, 65 (top), 86, 90, 94-95, 96, 97, 98-99, 100-101, 103, 110, 116, 118-119, 122, 123, 124, 126, 136, 137, 138-139, 151, 154-155, 160, 166, 169, 172-173, 174, 175, 176, 177, 178, 179 (bottom), 183, 192, 193, 200, 205, 210, 211, 240, 250, 253

© **Jordi Miralles**
pg. 14, 17, 24-25, 30, 34, 66-67, 70, 73, 106, 150, 161, 196, 219, 241

© **Pepe Escoda**
pg. 15, 21, 22, 23, 29, 41, 93, 170, 171, 179 (top)

© **Yael Pincus**
pg. 39, 40, 42, 45(top), 63, 68-69, 74-75, 157, 246-248, 249, 251(top), 251(bottom)

© **Jose Luis Hausmann**
pg. 48-49, 168, 228, 229, 230-231, 234-235, 236, 248

© **Andrea Martiradonna**
pg. 59, 117

© **Tuca Reinés**
pg. 58 (bottom)

© **Carlos Dominguez**
pg. 26-27, 121, 128-129, 171, 142-143

© **Tapeten der 70's**
pg. 28, 36-37, 45(bottom), 52, 56-57, 76, 127, 135

© **Hideyuki Yamashita**
pg. 206-207

© **Alno AG**
pg. 46-47, 198-199

© **Ikea**
pg. 252

© **Toscoquattro**
pg. 148, 186, 237 (bottom)

© **Reto Guntlli**
pg. 242-243, 244

© **Bonaldo**
pg. 131

© **Carlos Tobón**
pg. 201

© **Undine Pröhl**
pg. 35, 184-185

© **Andy Birchall**
pg. 140

© **CCAfrica**
pg. 152-153, 158-159

© **Flaminia**
pg. 182

© **Parmesso**
pg. 71

© **Farshid Assassi**
pg. 232, 233, 237 (top)

arbara Karant
188

icardo Labougle
87, 92

eramag
215, 218

lan Williams
107, 190-191, 226-227

irginia del Guidice
212-213

ersace Ceramic Design
180-181

XIA, designer Lino Codato
216-217

anotta Spa
65 (bottom), 78, 204

oberto Constantini
214, 220-221

arim Rashid
84-85

oche Bobois
80-81, 83, 104, 197, 245 (top),
5 (bottom)

atrick Engquist
225

© La Oca
pg. 60-61, 62, 108-109, 111, 112-113, 130,
132-133, 156, 194-195, 202,208-209

© estudi hac
pg. 72, 134

© Bisazza
pg. 189

© Duravit
pg. 102, 120

© John Bennett
pg. 222, 224